Ten Myths
about

MICHAEL GREEN
AND GORDON CARKNER

A LION BOOK

Published by
Lion Publishing plc
Sandy Lane West, Oxford, England
ISBN 0 7459 1441 1
Albatross Books Pty Ltd
PO Box 320, Sutherland, NSW 2232, Australia
ISBN 0 86760 995 8

First edition 1988
10 9 8 7 6 5 4

Acknowledgments
Photographs by Susanna Burton, pages 17, 52–53, 72–73, 77;
Sally and Richard Greenhill, page 57; Sefton Photo Library,
page 17; David Townsend, 4, 24–25, 36–37, 64–65; ZEFA,
page 12–13, 32, 45

This book was inspired by and is in part based upon a privately
distributed booklet and poster display called *Ten Myths About
Christianity*. These were written and produced by Gordon Carkner,
Herbert Gruning, J. Richard Middleton and Bruce Toombs in 1983.
A second edition was produced and copyrighted in 1984. Permission
was granted by these authors for the more expanded writing of the
present illustrated book. The poster set is available from IVCF of
Canada, 1840 Lawrence Ave E., Scarborough, Ontario, Canada
M1R 2Y4.

Printed and bound in Slovenia

CONTENTS

TEN MYTHS ABOUT CHRISTIANITY
THE WORLD WE LIVE IN

'It was the best of times: it was the worst of times.' These words of Charles Dickens to describe the years of the French Revolution fit our own day remarkably well. Yes, it is the best of times: would you prefer to have lived in any other century? The fantastic advances in science and technology, the control of disease and the length of life, the comfort of homes and the ease of travel in what has become a global village. . . It would all have been undreamed-of even a hundred years ago.

But it is no less the worst of times. There has never been such a threat to life on this planet as there is today. Never has there been such rape of our world's resources, never such famine, so many deaths by torture. The injustice in society, the breakdown of marriage, the abuse of wives and children, the absence of values, and the inhuman way we treat each other are breathtaking in a world that considers itself civilized. The Russian joke is very near the bone: 'Under capitalism man exploits man. Under communism the reverse is true'! Underneath all the surface ills of our society there is a profound loss of identity and purpose. Who am I? Where is the world going? What really matters? What will last?

Is Christian faith a real possibility in the modern technological world?

The old remedies for the human condition have been found wanting. The optimism of the humanists? Shattered on the rock of two bestial world wars and the continual carnage in world society. Marxism's economic restructuring? Human hearts remain as unfulfilled beyond the Berlin Wall as in Manhattan. Materialism? Utterly selfish, and utterly unsatisfying - some of the richest people in the world are the most unhappy. Dr Ronald Conway, a leading Australian psychiatrist, wrote of Melbourne society what is true of many 'first-world' countries: 'We have in parts of Melbourne the highest barbiturate dependence in the world, the highest suicide rate among young males between eighteen and thirty, the highest declared rate of rape in the world, and one in four women and one in ten men are suffering from depression. Australians have everything, and yet they have nothing to live for.' Where, then, shall we look for an answer to the most profound questions of our lives and our society? Is there any guidance to be had? Are there any values that will last?

During the height of the Roman Empire, at the crossroads of Greek, Roman and Jewish culture, Jesus of Nazareth was born. His life and teaching, his death and rumoured resurrection have captured the hearts and minds of millions all over the world during the past two thousand years, and today a third of the world's population claims to follow him.

Here was his Manifesto:

'The Spirit of the Lord is upon me,

Because he has appointed me to preach
good news to the poor.
He has sent me to proclaim release
to the captives
And the recovery of sight
to the blind,
To set at liberty the oppressed,
And to proclaim the year of
the Lord's favour.'

He claims that he has come to bring the answer to
the human condition, reconcile the estranged, and
bring hope to the most despairing. So immensely
valuable are we to God that Jesus has come to show
us what God is like, and to call for our commitment.
As we surrender ourselves to that undeserved love,
we shall discover what life is all about and what
human beings were made for. That is the claim,
no less. But is it credible that this individual from
2,000 years ago can have anything to say to our
modern world? Can today's rootless, emotionally-
wounded men and women find any reason for hope
in Jesus of Nazareth? We believe they can. Many
thousands of people every day across the world are
entrusting their lives to this Jesus, mostly in Africa, Asia and Latin America. Properly understood,
and personally trusted, he remains the only hope
for mankind.

But Jesus had been obscured by Christianity. And
myths cluster around him like barnacles on the
bottom of a ship after a long voyage. This book
attempts to scrape off the barnacles, to explode the
myths, and to enable you to make your considered
response to the real Jesus. The ten myths we have

chosen are not arbitrary. They represent what a great many people think and say. Because they insulate people from the real Jesus, they need to be ripped away. If we are to accept Jesus we need to be clear what we are accepting. If we reject him, we need to be equally clear what it is we are rejecting, and why. It is the aim of this little book to make the issues crystal clear.

MYTH 1

JESUS CHRIST WAS ONLY A GREAT MORAL TEACHER

Jesus of Nazareth is the most important figure
the world has ever known. This Galilean peasant
teacher has had more influence on mankind than
any other person. We date our era by him. Our
educational system, our values, our standards, our
laws, our medicine and our love of justice and
freedom owe more to him than to any other
source. Art, music, sculpture, thought, literature
has been more taken up with Jesus than with any
other topic during the past two thousand years.
Yet he is for all practical purposes ignored, except
by a small minority. He is inconvenient. His very
name makes us uncomfortable. And so he is
condescendingly dismissed with a wave of the hand
and the comment, 'Jesus? Yes, of course, he was a
great moral teacher'.

Now undoubtedly he was a great moral teacher - one
in a class of his own. He spoke with great authority:
'You have heard it said, but I tell you. . . ' He
spoke with great simplicity, so that ordinary people
could understand him. He taught with remarkable
depth: 'Love your enemies, do good to those who
mistreat you' is a highly controversial and costly but
exceedingly effective way of dealing with violent
opposition. His wisdom silenced opponents time
and again: 'Render to Caesar the things that are
Caesar's and to God the things that are God's' has
proved to be an utterly original and unanswerable

bulwark against totalitarianism, and also the guideline for Christians in public affairs. His teaching was embarrassingly specific and highly relevant to daily life: 'Go and do likewise' said Jesus at the conclusion of his most uncomfortable parable of the Good Samaritan.

No wonder people marvelled at the teaching of this man who lacked a higher education. No wonder they followed him everywhere, hanging on his words. 'No one ever taught like this,' they said, and they were right.

But something else is remarkable about Jesus and his teaching. As well as teaching the highest standards known to mankind, he actually kept them. He not only taught people to love their enemies, but also forgave those who crucified him. He did not only call people to lay down their life for their friends, but actually did it. He not only taught that it was blessed to be poor - he lived that way. It makes him the most remarkable of all teachers. Here was one who taught the most exciting standards, and actually embodied them.

Yes, Jesus was a great moral teacher. But neither he nor his followers will allow us to get away with the idea that he was that and no more. Jesus was either something very much more or very much less. He made the most astonishing claims, claims that have never been paralleled by any sane person. He claimed that he could forgive people's sins, that he had the right to people's worship, that he alone represented the way to God, the truth of God and the life of God, that he had come to seek and save the lost, that he would give his life as a ransom for many, that he would rise from the dead, and that on the day of judgment humanity would be accountable to him. (It is worth looking at the places in the Gospels where he says these things: Mark 2:5; John 20:28, 14:6; Luke 19:10; Mark 10:45; Matthew 17:9, 7:21-25.)

To be sure, Jesus did not go round saying 'I am God'. That would have been utterly misleading and totally incomprehensible. But, as Elton Trueblood put it, 'All four Gospels bristle with supernatural claims on the part of Jesus. If he was only a teacher, he was a very misleading one.' The claims came not only explicitly in verses such as those above, but implicitly as he fulfilled prophecy, performed actions ascribing to God alone in the Old Testament, and worked miracles. The claim to bring God Almighty into our world, to call people to God by calling them to himself, confronts us on almost every page of the Gospels. It is part of the very fabric of the New Testament writings. It convinced some of the most determined and unshakeable monotheists in the world, Jews to a man. It convinced sceptics, political leaders, prostitutes, fishermen and tax collectors like the earliest disciples, and violent opponents like the brilliant and fanatical adversary Saul of Tarsus who became the most ardent believer. It has convinced billions of people all over the world ever since.

To say Jesus was simply a good moral teacher is untenable. It means ignoring half the evidence. If he is not the one who makes God real to us

by sharing our human nature, he is either an untrustworthy liar or a deluded imbecile.

But why should we believe his claims? Many have made false claims for themselves. Many psychiatric hospitals contain deluded individuals. It is, and it ought to be, very difficult to think of Jesus as more than a man. And yet what are the alternatives?

• Was he a sham? But is it credible that this man who was so ruthless against hypocrisy should have built his whole ministry on a lie? Is it possible that

Jesus' first followers, tough fishermen among them, were convinced he was more than just a great teacher.

he would have allowed himself to be executed in the most excruciating of deaths for what he knew was untrue?

● Or was he simply mistaken? That will hardly do. If the greatest teacher of all is mistaken about the central issue of his life and claims, he is not such a great teacher after all. If we decline to credit what he has to say about his origin and authority, why should we pay any attention to the rest of his teaching?

• Did Jesus perhaps suffer delusions of grandeur? Maybe this carpenter-teacher had ideas above his station, and his claims to deity were the results of some mental imbalance? That position is hard to substantiate. There are normally three key symptoms in those who are mentally ill. They have gross inadequacy in relating to the real world; they display gross inadequacy in personal relationships; and they are marked by gross inadequacy in communication. One has only to mention those three symptoms to see that they are each utterly inapplicable to Jesus, the supreme communicator, the man who possessed the most devastating insight into reality and was of all men the most loving and strong in personal relations. There is no trace of fanaticism or mental imbalance about him.

Jesus of Nazareth was not simply a great moral teacher. He cuts too deep and steps out too far from the crowd for that. We can call him a liar if we think we can sustain such a charge. We can cast doubts on his mental state. But the tag of 'only a great moral teacher' does not fit.

It was never an option in his own day. Some of his contemporaries thought him mad, others loved him. But he never seems to have received mild approval.

Neither is it an option for today. We have to shut him up or hear him out. The sheer impact of his person and his claims forces us to make up our minds. What are we to think of this great moral teacher who makes such impossible claims? Could he be right after all?

MYTH 2

CHRISTIANITY STIFLES
PERSONAL FREEDOM

'Freedom' is the prevailing cry of the twentieth
century, at individual and at national level. It is
also an overwhelming psychological preoccupation
in the West.

Yet for so central an idea it has been left curiously
undefined. Often freedom is seen very superficially, as the removal of immediate constraints
without thinking where this autonomy will all lead.
Frequently it leads to abuse. Liberty turns into
licence, and is used for merely selfish ends. Heady
wine though it is, freedom can produce some very
painful hangovers.

Yet freedom of the right kind is essential for our
humanity. So if, as some believe, Christianity stifles
our freedom, then it should be resisted.

At the same time, it is strange that Christianity
should be thought an enemy of freedom. After
all, it is Christianity which has so often stood
up for the poor and oppressed, the captive and
the underprivileged. Liberation from ignorance,
disease and political subjugation has resulted time
and again where Christian faith and principles
have been brought to bear. So why should it
seem repressive?

Part of the answer lies simply in the selfishness
of our hearts. We want our own way. We see God

Faith in Jesus sets us free from the limitations of our particular culture and circumstances – free to be the people God created.

as a celestial policeman and we want to run away from him and thumb our noses at his regulations. We want to do our own thing. And it is obvious that allegiance to Jesus Christ will put some limits on this freedom.

Another part is the sad reality of legalistic Christians. A lot of Christians seem to have developed an extensive list of do's and don'ts which seem both stupid and petty. If Christianity means submitting to bourgeois legalism, then no thank you.

But at a deeper level, the answer lies in the wide assumption that there are no standards which have absolute claim on us. Facts are one thing, as many think, such as scientific facts. But values are entirely subjective. You take your pick in the ethical supermarket of life, and you don't complain when others select different values.

'The greatest question of our time is not communism versus individualism; not East versus West; it is whether man can bear to live without God in an age which has killed him.' So writes the historian Will Durant. The point is a powerful one. Most people in the Western lands live as if God is dead. If that is so, ethics can only derive from human custom or from personal choice. And therein lies the problem.

As Woody Allen put it in his inimitable way, 'More than at any time in history, mankind stands at a crossroad. One path leads to despair and utter hopelessness; the other leads to total extinction. Let us pray that we have the wisdom to choose correctly!'

Or, in the more prosaic words of the moralist Mark Hanna, 'The importance of moral experience can hardly be overestimated, for today the human race stands at the brink of self-destruction. It is not first of all technology but moral decision-making that will determine whether or not we have a future, and if so, what kind of future it will be.'

Hanna is right. If morals are simply a matter of headcount, if values are all relative and depend on personal choice, the world is heading for destruction. Dr Paul Johnson, the British historian, writes, 'What is so notable about the twentieth century and a principal cause of its horrors is that great physical power has been acquired by men who have no fear of God and who believe themselves restrained by no absolute code of conduct.'

If there are no absolute values, then what is our basis for distinguishing between Mother Teresa and Adolf Hitler? Why should it be thought better to save the lives of castaways in the streets of Calcutta than to murder six million people in gas chambers? But the moment you admit that one course of action is without qualification better than another, you admit the existence of an absolute standard by which you are judging.

Alexander Solzhenitsyn, in his celebrated address in Harvard, showed how shallow is the popular philosophy of hedonism, having a good time as the goal of life. 'If humanism were right in declaring that man is born to be happy, he would not have to die. But since he is born to die, his task on earth must be of a more spiritual nature. . . so that one may leave this life a better human being than when one started it.'

Freedom, then, must be about more than choosing our code of conduct. It is to do with the kind of people we are. Jesus of Nazareth strikes me as the most liberated man who ever lived. He knew very well there was a divinely appointed standard of ethics, and he framed his life in accordance with it. He said, 'I do always those things which please him (God)'. But could anyone say that his faith stifled his freedom? He was utterly free of covetousness, free of hypocrisy, free of the fear of others, free to be himself. He was free to look into people's hearts and tell them the truth about themselves, free to love men and women with warmth and purity, and free at the end voluntarily to surrender his life for others.

Was there ever so free a human being? Yet he had discovered the truth that freedom is not the licence to do what you want but the liberation to do what you ought. He has shown that real freedom is unselfish and warm, generous and person-centred, more to do with relationships than rule-keeping. Jesus is the free person's model. Duty did not stifle him. Obedience did not obliterate his freedom. Circumstances did not imprison him. He was utterly free - free to use his power for others, free to love the unlovely, free to confront oppressors and injustice. The ultimate liberated man.

And true Christian freedom is Jesus-shaped. There is no sniff of legalism about it. It is based on the conviction that there is indeed an absolute in the realm of ethics, and that this ideal is not unknown to us. It has been given personal embodiment in Jesus of Nazareth. So Christian freedom is nothing to do with rules and regulations. It is everything to do with pleasing Christ and allowing him to be the model for our relationships with God and our fellows, for our service of others, for our standards of honesty and purity. It is allowing the best human being who ever lived to be the inspiration for our living. What is stifling about that? To be sure, it may often run against the way of our selfish indulgence: but that is necessary in any pursuit of excellence. It applies to the athlete, the academic, the doctor.

Christian freedom stands irrespective of our circumstances. It progressively releases us to be the kind of human being that in our best moments we want to be. And it results in the sort of behaviour which, if universalized, would not destroy society but transform it.

In a word, the only freedom which Christianity stifles is the freedom to injure ourselves and other people. True freedom only comes from Jesus.

MYTH 3

CHRISTIANITY IS JUST A CRUTCH FOR THE WEAK

Some people pride themselves in their strength. They feel almost invincible. And so they can easily despise a faith that speaks of strengthening the weak and lifting up the fallen.

'I don't need Christianity,' they say, 'It's just a crutch for the weaklings!'

I have often heard a sneer like that. And I wonder how the young person, full of health and scorn who utters it, would feel if he or she fell downstairs and broke a leg. I guess that person's attitude to crutches might change!

Perhaps we have grown so accustomed to the crutches of our society that we hardly recognize them for what they are. The mad quest for intimacy, to still the ever-present pain of loneliness. The activism with which we fill our lives because we dare not stop and ask who we are and where we are going. The dependence on alcohol and drugs because the pressures around and within us have got too great. The anxiety state which demands an array of tranquillizers before we can face going to sleep at night. The attempt to prop up our lives with material things. Or the reaction which drives us to Eastern mysticism and seminars for the improvement of our human potential. Crutches, every one of them.

Other props are less obvious but just as much

crutches for the weak: power over other people, fame, wealth, beauty. There seems no end to the props people use as they go limping through life.

And Christianity - is it just another crutch?

In one sense, yes it is. Christianity is for people who do not pretend they are invincible, but know they have got something broken. If ours were a perfect world and we were perfect people there might be no need for Christianity. But such is not the case. Our world, our lives are fractured by greed and lust, by cruelty and selfishness. Don't believe me. Just glance at a newspaper or watch the television news.

Christianity is unashamedly a rescue religion. That is why so many self-satisfied people steer clear of it. 'I have come to heal the sick,' said Jesus. 'Those who are well don't need a doctor.' But he knew that in his meaning no one is healthy. Not even you or me.

As George Orwell put it tartly in *Nineteen Eighty Four*, 'We have found the enemy: it is us'. But most of us won't even admit our injuries, obvious though they are to everybody else. Unless we do, we shall have to continue to hobble through life. Our makeshift crutches will not bear our weight. We need radical healing. And that is precisely what Jesus Christ offers.

Set side by side two estimates of human nature. We think we have hearts of gold. But the prophet Jeremiah said, 'The heart is deceitful above all things and desperately corrupt.' Which evaluation is closer to the mark?

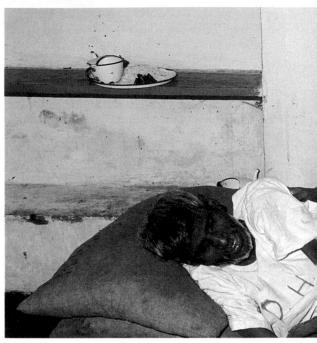

Think how often in the course of the day our words let us down: bitter words, hasty words, filthy words, cruel words, lying words. Think how often we have reason to be ashamed of our actions: greedy, unfair, self-centred, thoughtless, cruel actions, very often. And how about our characters? I wonder how those who work with us and under us would assess those? As for our thoughts - which of us would not blush to the roots of our hair if our thoughts could be flashed onto a television screen for all to see?

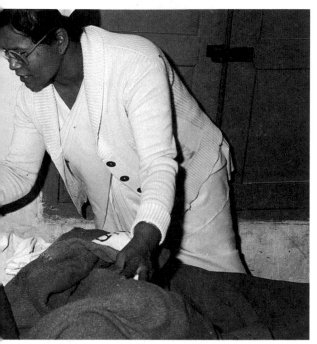

Christian faith can certainly help us when we most need help. But Jesus meets us in our strength as well as in our weakness.

How does God react to all this? By pretending it does not matter? Of course it matters. The evil in our lives spoils our characters, it ruins relationships, and it alienates us from him. Moreover it has an uncanny grip on us. Which of us does not long to be free of the moral weakness which pulls us down?

The Christian good news is that God has acted to restore the situation. He has come to this world to show us what he is really like, to show us how we could live life at its best.

But that isn't all. He came to build a bridge over the troubled waters of our alienation and selfishness. He came to construct a road back to God. And he did this, against all human logic, by laying down his life for us. Our wickedness had erected an impenetrable barrier between us and God. When Jesus died on the cross he broke through the barrier, even though its masonry fell on him and killed him. He picked up the tab for our debts, all of us. He took responsibility for the evil and wickedness of the whole wide world, drained its poison and wiped the slate clean. And he could do so, fittingly, because he was God as well as man. 'God was in Christ, reconciling the world to himself.' And because he did so each one of us can face God with an uncondemning conscience, our debts paid.

What is more, even death could not hold Jesus down. He rose again on the first Easter Day. He is alive, and Christians claim not just to know about him but to know him in personal encounter. They are convinced that this risen Christ gives them the power to overcome habits which previously had pulled them down time after time.

It is, therefore, a radical reshaping of human nature that Christianity offers. It liberates us from the shackles of the past, and sets us free to be the people we were intended to be. It enables us to make the contribution towards other people and society at large which we know to be right, but which, because of our unhealed self-centredness, we never actually got round to.

I suppose you could say that the wood of the cross is like a splint for our fractured lives. But that splint is applied with the intention of effecting a cure, to enable us to stand and walk and run.

See what happens to some of the 'weak' who avail themselves of this 'crutch'.

• A Mother Teresa comes out of her nunnery to love the helpless and homeless on the streets of Calcutta.

• A David Sheppard, international athlete with a glittering future, gives his life to serve the needs of the inner city, first as clergyman then as bishop.

• A Chuck Colson, ruthless self-seeking lawyer and presidential aide who had a share in the guilt to Watergate, gives the rest of his life to seeking social and political justice in the name of Christ and ministering to the needs of prisoners.

• A George Foreman, former heavyweight boxing champion of the world, whose scarred face is now full of the love of Christ, might mutter gently in your ear, 'What was that I heard you say - that Christianity is a crutch for the weak?'

• An Alexander Solzhenitsyn, rotting in the Gulag and surrendering his whole intellect and being to the Jesus who lived and died and rose for him, gains the strength to challenge a totalitarian regime on behalf of human dignity and freedom.

And those are just samples from the millions who have thrown away the pathetic crutches with which they used to limp along the road of life. They have come for healing to the seasoned wood of the cross, and they have been transformed.

If you think Christianity is a crutch for the weak, make sure that your accusation is not a smokescreen to deny your own inadequacies. Make sure that it is not an excuse to evade the claims that the living God has on your life. His remedy is very radical, but very effective. He takes wounded, fractured people and makes them whole.

MYTH 4

PEOPLE BECOME CHRISTIANS THROUGH SOCIAL CONDITIONING

Only a fool would claim that cultural circumstances play no part at all in people's religious beliefs.

We are all affected greatly by our heredity and our environment, and particularly by friends whose opinions we value. Nobody would deny that a Hindu environment predisposes you towards Hinduism, a Christian one to Christianity and so forth. But the question is, do heredity and environment constitute a complete explanation of why people believe and behave as they do? That is altogether more questionable.

A 'Christian' background may put you off Christianity. A great many children in Sunday schools revolt by the age of eleven, and sometimes children of clergy families determine in their teens to have nothing more to do with organized religion. How does this fact, and fact it is, square with the assertion that conversion and religious experience are the result, and only the result, of social conditioning?

More often still, it works the other way. Many millions of people in the Soviet Union and in China these days are becoming Christians, in the teeth of sustained opposition by the authorities. Soviet prisons are full of Christians who are certainly not there because they are socially conditioned towards the faith. Everything in their environment inclines them in the direction of atheism and dialectical materialism. Yet Communism has been totally unable to stop the growth of Christian conversions in these two great lands. Interesting, isn't it? A great revival of Christianity is taking place today in the strictly communist country of Rumania. Who is going to tell me that this is due to social conditioning?

Perhaps even more impressive are the Sawi tribes-people whom Don Richardson, a pioneer missionary, describes in his *Peace Child*. Their culture was so corrupt that every single human virtue was deemed a vice among them, and deception was thought the highest virtue. When they heard the story of Jesus for the first time they cheered the treachery of Judas Iscariot. He was the hero! There is a very flourishing Christian community there now. Social conditioning? Tell me another!

This same argument about social conditioning is regularly applied to conscience. So far from supplying a categorical imperative in our lives, telling us which is the right way to go, conscience is seen by atheist philosophers as merely the reflection of social pressures on us. Naturally, conscience is affected to some extent by the society in which we live, but that cannot be a full explanation. Most of the moral advances in history have been brought about by passionate reformers who stood boldly out against the pressures of their society because of what their conscience told them was right. Think of the liberation of slaves, of women, of children condemned to fifteen hours a day in the factories, of prisoners chained day and night to the walls of their cells. In every case reform was brought about on strictly conscientious grounds, and in every case in the teeth of the opposition of society and its standards at the time. Conscience is no lackey of social conditioning.

But if social reasons lie behind what some people believe, then they explain atheism as well as other creeds. Paul Vitz, a noted Christian psychologist, was brought up as a Christian. Then at eighteen he abandoned his heritage and became an atheist. At thirty-eight, by now a professor of psychology, he re-investigated Christianity, came to the conclusion it was true, and committed his life to Christ. He now declares that his reasons for adopting atheism were 'superficial, irrational, and largely without intellectual and moral integrity'. He did it in order to win favour with his peers.

Christian conversion is much misunderstood. It is regarded as sudden, irrational, selective, if not downright illusory. But what are its essential elements?

They may perhaps best be seen in the archetype of all Christian conversions, that of Saul of Tarsus. While much of the paraphernalia of his conversion was unique, four elements stand out which are present in every authentic conversion.

● It touched his conscience. He knew that he was kicking against the goads.

Religious beliefs are deeply affected by cultural surroundings. Yet there must be more to faith than cultural influence, or how can we explain conversion in today's secular society?

● It touched his understanding. He realized that the Jesus he was persecuting was the risen Messiah and Son of God.

● It touched his will. He came to the point of giving in to Jesus and beginning to follow him.

● It changed his whole life - his ambitions, his character, his relationships, his whole perspective on life. No conversion can claim to be real unless it embodies these four elements.

But what if the whole thing is an illusion? What if Freud was right in regarding religious experience itself as illusory? There are, I believe, three tests which it is proper to apply if you are wondering whether religious experience in general and Christianity in particular is illusory.

First, the test of history. This does not apply to all religions; only to those that make historical claims. But it is most certainly the case with Christianity. It revolves entirely around the person and death and supposed resurrection of Jesus of Nazareth, a carpenter-teacher who lived under Roman occupation of Palestine in the first third of the first century AD. There is nothing illusory about Jesus, nor is there in the impact he had on his contemporaries and all subsequent generations the world over. His life of love and integrity, of courage and insight is unparalleled. There is nothing illusory about his claims (*see* myth 1). His death was real enough, and widely witnessed. And his resurrection is extremely well attested (*see* myth 8). Nor could anyone doubt the reality of the church that has sprung from Jesus and now claims many millions of adherents throughout the world. It simply makes no sense to argue that Christian faith is illusory, the product of social conditioning. It is rooted in history. Its founder and origins will survive the most searching scrutiny.

Second, there is the test of character. When drunkards become sober and crooks become honest, when animists lose their bondage to the spirit world and people enslaved by black magic are set free, when self-centred people become generous - well, it is very difficult to put the reason for all this down to illusion. The transformation of people's lives is not the only criterion of authenticity, but it has been very impressive among Christians down the centuries.

Third, there is the test of power. That is another criterion of the validity of religious experience. All that we know about delusions and obsessional neuroses is that they tend towards the disintegration of character, unbalanced behaviour and the inability to achieve goals. But Christianity has precisely the opposite effect. It makes people whole. And its power continues through life and in the face of death - when many delusions are stripped away.

None of these three tests is attributable to social conditioning. The social-conditioning theory cannot explain historical facts or the deep change in people's characters. As an explanation of the power of Christianity it will not do.

MYTH 5

CHRISTIANS ARE OTHERWORLDLY AND IRRELEVANT TO MODERN LIFE

This is often said, but hard to understand. Most Christians today could do with being more concerned with the hereafter, not less. In a previous generation heaven and hell loomed large in the minds of believers, but today many professing Christians seem rather less than preoccupied with life after death.

This is a pity, because history shows that the people who have done most for this world are those who have been most sure about the next. Think of Augustine, who sat down as the barbarians were surging like a rising tide into the Roman Empire, and wrote a book called *The City of God* which inspired leading thinkers for the next thousand years. Reformers such as Luther and Calvin had their heads in heaven, you might think. But the effects on earth shook the whole of Europe.

If your horizon is bounded by this world, you have no star to steer by. You cannot reach beyond your very circumscribed personal world to find any larger perspective. But if you believe in the living God, who made this world but is not bound by it, then your outlook changes radically. You see history as moving towards a goal. You gain some glimpse of the ideal by which this world can be judged and

towards which you can seek to move society.
The coming of Jesus links this world to the next. He
is the kingdom of God in person. And as people are
committed to him, so they enlist in the furthering of
that kingdom on earth. There is no romantic idealism about this. People are sick of utopias which
disappoint (the literal meaning of the Greek word
utopia is 'nowhere-land'). What Christians are concerned with is highly relevant to this world and its
needs, for the very simple reason that they know

People living in today's great cities need to rediscover the spiritual dimension to life.

God shares that concern. He proved it by coming in Jesus, dying for us and rising from the tomb on the first Easter Day. God could not have done more to show he is involved, up to the neck. And so Christians, in their turn, are committed to getting involved in bringing the values and standards, the love and concerns, the justice and truthfulness of the Age to Come into this age here and now. They know it will never be complete. There is no starry-eyed idealism about them. They see themselves as an embassy of heaven, living out the life of their parent state in a foreign land whose good they seek to promote. Perhaps only otherworldly people can really do much earthly good.

But if Christians today could use a bit more other-worldliness, their faith is certainly not irrelevant.

If ever there was a need for Christian values and motivation, surely it is now. The perils of a world where the doom clock points at six minutes to midnight; the carnage in scores of conflicts all over the globe; the decimation wrought by famine of unimagined proportions; the social violence, the disregard of the individual, the widespread oppression - all these things make the need for Christian involvement greater than ever before. Do we not need the Christian charities to respond to the natural disasters in the world? Do we not need the Tutus and the Solzhenitsyns to plead the cause of justice in countries like South Africa and the Soviet Union? And who is going to do it unless it is those who have some Archimedean point outside their own society from which to speak in the name of truth, compassion and justice? Why is it that Christian doctors can serve in the most primitive situations, where others without a Christian faith are not often found?

Once you are captivated by the self-sacrifice of Jesus, you cannot insulate yourself from the world of need he came to minister to. If you believe that human beings really matter, as children of God, then you are simply bound to get involved with them for their welfare.

'It is a serious thing', wrote C.S. Lewis, 'to live in a society of potential god and goddesses. . . It is immortals whom we joke with, work with, marry, snub, exploit - immortal horrors or everlasting splendours.'

That is the logic behind Christian social involvement. And whenever the tide of faith sweeps in, there is always a corresponding rise in social concern and service to the community, as happened in England in the nineteenth century. Almost every aspect of social reform was brought about, not by the agnostic followers of John Stuart Mill, but by men and women brought to a living faith through the revivals that had so profoundly affected the country. The Great Reform Bill was brought in largely through the influence of Christian parliamentarians. The Earl of Shaftesbury was responsible for the Mines Act, forbidding women and children to be forced to work down the mines, the Factories Act limiting hours of work, and so forth. Dr Barnardo founded homes for orphans. Elizabeth Fry brought about prison reform. Josephine Butler got Parliament to outlaw child prostitution and protect women. And of course Wilberforce, a little earlier, had lived to see his lifelong struggle for the abolition of slavery crowned with success.

All these people acted so effectively and passionately in this world because they were so clear about the next. They had come to a living faith in Christ, and because of it they were nerved to serve him in practical ways for the good of others whom he had made. The same is true of men like Martin Luther King Jr, Mother Teresa and a horde of others in our own day.

All of them were persuaded that the atheist account of the world was profoundly wrong. We are not, as Jean-Paul Sartre maintained, 'an empty bubble on the sea of nothingness'. If you believe that, then there is no good reason to put yourself out for other people. But if you believe we are made in the image of God, so valuable that Christ died for us, then you roll up your sleeves and get involved. That is what real Christianity requires. And that is what Christians at their best have always done.

MYTH 6

SCIENCE IS IN CONFLICT WITH CHRISTIAN FAITH

Top scientists do not make this claim, but ordinary people often do. For them science deals with facts, Christianity with values and emotions. Science can be proved, they say, while Christianity cannot. Science is progressive: Christianity has often opposed progress. The scientific method is logical: Christianity involves the leap of faith. Science deals with the laws of nature: Christianity, apparently, thrives on miracle. The contrasts are immense.

Immense they may appear, but they are myths all the same. Let's look at them one by one.

● Is it true that science deals with facts, Christianity with values and emotions? No. Both deal with evidence. Science deals with the evidence about our world which is presented by what we can see, touch, measure and calculate. Christianity deals with what we can infer about our world from the life, teaching, death and resurrection of Jesus. He is very much open to examination - by the science of history. His life and teaching, his death and resurrection are well attested. They are proper subjects for careful enquiry. The conclusions we reach will have far-reaching implications for how we see the world.

Certainly Christianity involves value judgments, but so does science. Both involve the agent as well as the object. Both have a subjective as well as an objective side. There is no such thing as an uninterpreted fact. Even emotions are common to both 'scientists' and 'Christian believers'. Both are human beings. Both are reluctant to accept evidence which goes against what they have always believed.

The astronomer Robert Jastrow details the hurt and angry feelings of astronomer after astronomer at the implications of the Big-Bang theory of cosmic origins. This now-dominant theory fits well with creation at some point in time and space - with a Creator. And for some who have held out as unbelievers that is totally unacceptable. 'It cannot really be true,' writes Allan Sandage. 'I would like to reject it,' writes Phillip Morrison. 'The notion of a beginning is repugnant to me,' writes Eddington. Yes, science deals with values and emotions no less than Christianity.

• Then is it true that science can be proved, but Christianity cannot? Again no. Science cannot be 'proved'. The heart of the scientific method is empiricism, allowing the evidence to lead you where it will. Very well, if that is so, it is obvious that you cannot prove any scientific hypothesis. It is a product of observed uniformities. But it would only require one contrary instance to bring the whole thing down. For centuries Newton's theories seemed to be proven. . . and then along came Einstein.

To prove a thing with certainty, you have to show that it follows inexorably from something already known. Only deductive knowledge is certain. Of course, for all practical purposes we accept the reliability of 'laws' discovered by the sciences. But they are not proved.

Equally, you cannot prove Christianity. You cannot show there is someone greater than God from whom he can with certainty be deduced. That would be a contradiction in terms, for 'God' is the name we give to the *ultimate* being. You cannot prove the historicity and teaching of Jesus Christ. You can't do it with Julius Caesar either. Historical events are not 'proved'. They are accepted or not on the ground of competent, credible, and preferably contemporary testimony. That is the ground on which Christians ask acceptance of Jesus.

• Is science progressive, then, while Christianity opposes progress? There is some truth in that. But only some. Christianity has been opposed to progress at times in its history. You can think of the Orthodox Church in Tsarist Russia. Or of the Spanish Inquisition. Or of the church's opposition of Copernicus and Galileo at the dawn of scientific discovery. Or of ecclesiastical opposition to Darwin later on. Not at all good.

But often Christianity has been in the van of progress. Progress in education, in medicine, in the liberation of the oppressed, of prisoners, of slaves, of women. And remember the many Christians in at the start of modern science - Kepler, Priestley, Harvey. . .

Remember, too, the dark side of science. Think of nuclear fission - neutral in itself but opening the door to the destruction of the planet. Think of the terrifying possibilities opening up through biological engineering and chemical warfare. You might call these things 'progress' in terms of strict academic science. But do they represent advance and progress for humanity itself?

● Well then, is the scientific method logical, while Christianity involves the leap of faith? That is another myth. There is, of course, a logic and an order in scientific enquiry; there is also an order and a logic in the philosophical, historical, ethical and religious disciplines of Christianity. But as a matter of fact, both depend in the long run on faith. Faith is not believing what you know is not true, as one schoolboy defined it. Faith is self-commitment on the basis of evidence. And that is fundamental both to the scientific method and to the Christian faith.

You can't do without faith to begin either scientific study or Christian living. In both cases you need to commit yourself. In the case of science, you must commit yourself to the assumption that the world we see and touch is real, though there are grave problems in that assumption as every philosopher knows. You have to commit yourself to belief in the uniformity of nature and the prevalence of cause and effect. Without these prior 'leaps of faith', reasonable though they are, you cannot begin science.

Science and faith are often spoken of as if we have to choose to base life on one or the other. But in fact we need both.

Equally, real Christianity involves commitment. Commitment to the assumption that there is a living God who has revealed himself in Jesus Christ. Commitment in faith to Jesus himself. Without that faith, that self-commitment on good evidence, there can be no Christianity.

In science, when you make a discovery, it is seldom by sheer thought or logic alone. There is that spark of imagination, that hunch, that experimentation. 'What if I were to try this..?'

There you have it. Self-commitment - on evidence. And if the experiment is successful you repeat it, and in due course it becomes an additional element in our knowledge. So it is with Christianity. The Christian claim is that God has not only made this world, but he has come to it. Christians then adopt the scientific method. They cannot know *a priori* if this claim is true. It is not a matter of sheer logic. They have to commit themselves to the hypothesis that it *could* be true and see if it *is*. They base their lives on the good evidence that certain things are true. And then they begin to discover that they *are* true: faith works.

Contrary to popular opinion, by far the greater number of those who are converted to Christianity in the universities are scientists. It is not all that surprising. The approach is so similar: self-commitment on evidence - or faith.

• And finally, what about miracle? If your theories are bounded by a closed physical universe with fixed and unalterable laws, you will find the concept of miracle, which involves the local and temporary suspension of those laws, intolerable. But that is a nineteenth century view of science, and you would find few scientists of stature supporting it. The whole scene is much more fluid since the discovery of quantum physics and Heisenberg's uncertainty principle. But the important point to remember is that 'laws of nature' are not prescriptive, but descriptive. They do not determine what may happen; they describe what normally does happen. Science can say that miracles do not usually occur in the ordinary course of nature. But it cannot legitimately claim they are impossible. Such a claim lies outside the limits of science. And if God has really come to this world in the person of Jesus Christ, is it so very surprising that miracles were worked by him, as the Gospels report? They cannot be ruled out as impossible. (They need to be carefully weighed for probability, but that is a very different matter.)

Science is not in conflict with the Christian faith. To be sure, some scientists are. Other scientists are passionately committed Christians, just like people in any other walk of life. The reasons for such decisions must be sought elsewhere than in science.

MYTH 7

THE BIBLE IS UNRELIABLE
AND CANNOT BE TRUSTED

The Bible is not a book at all. It is a library. It contains sixty-six books, written by an enormous variety of authors over a period of two thousand years in three languages. Some of the writers were Jews, some were not. Some were kings, some shepherds. The variety of literary genres in the Bible is kaleidoscopic: history and prophecy, psalms and poetry, Gospel and epistle, allegory and parable - even love story.

The really astonishing thing when you come to study the Bible is that, for all their diversity, the writers tell one story.

• You find the same view of God from the beginning of the Bible to the end. He is Creator, Saviour and Judge. He is holy love.

• You find the same understanding of human nature: capable of the greatest heights of goodness and the greatest depths of wickedness. Made to enjoy God but against him, our supreme good is to be reconciled to God and to one another.

• You find a common view of Jesus Christ. He is both God and man. A real human being like us, he nevertheless brought into our gaze the God we could not otherwise understand. His death on the cross is not simply a supreme example of heroism. It shows on one hand the depths of human wickedness, determined to eliminate the best when we see it, and on the other hand the depths of God's love, willing to go to any lengths to rescue us from the alienation we had chosen. The Bible writers are clear, too, that on the cross something deeply significant happened: 'He bore our sins in his own body on the tree.' They are no less clear that death was not strong enough to hold Jesus. He rose from the tomb on the first Easter Day. He is alive today, and we can encounter him. He can change our lives.

• You find the same hope. At the end of history God's purpose will be achieved on earth as it is in heaven.

There is no doubt that the biblical writers are united by the most astonishing harmony of outlook. I challenge anybody to find a parallel in history or · literature in the world. Where else would you find such unity about God among so vast a disparity of writers across two millennia?

Comparative religion is a very interesting study, in which we find humanity in search of God, and the different ends to that search. But the Bible is not really about humanity in search of God. It shows something much more surprising and radical: God in search of humanity. God is the supreme lover whom we have rejected, but he cares so much about us that he comes to find us, rebels though we are. There is no religion in the world that tells us anything comparable. But that theme, salvation, is the message of the Bible in its whole vast scope.

The Old Testament lies at the core of the three great monotheistic religions of the world: Judaism, Christianity and Islam. It cannot be airily swept aside as 'unreliable'. It is one of the seminal works of all mankind. You cannot, of course, prove the truth of what it says about God. That is a faith judgment. But you can show that the transmission of its text is extraordinarily reliable. The Dead Sea Scrolls, found in 1947, give the Hebrew text of a number of Old Testament books. Written between 150 BC and AD 70, they are 1,000 years older than any Hebrew manuscript of the Bible previously known. But the text is practically identical. It shows that we have extraordinarily reliable texts of the Old Testament.

And the Old Testament points beyond itself to a salvation which still lay in the future. As Augustine saw so clearly, the New Testament lies concealed in the Old and the Old is made clear in the New. And the centrepiece of the New Testament is Jesus himself, a first century Jew who was executed under the Roman governor Pontius Pilate.

There is secular evidence for Jesus. Two of the famous Roman writers of the period tell us about him, Tacitus (*Annals* 15.44) and Pliny the Younger (*Letters* 10.96). So do Jewish writings, Josephus (especially *Antiquities* 18.3.3) and the Mishnah. These texts attest his historicity, his unusual birth, his miracles, his teaching, his disciples, his messianic claims, his death by crucifixion, his claimed resurrection and his promised return at the end of history. There is also archaeological support, both that there were Christians and about what they believed, in the first century AD, and also for the trustworthiness of Christian statements in the Gospels and Acts.

But of course the main source of information available to us about Jesus is to be found in the New Testament itself. Can we trust it? That boils down to three issues:

• Can we trust the documents? Do we have the New Testament as it was written, or has the text been tampered with over the ages?

The answer is that the text of the New Testament is so sure that nobody makes conjectural emendations for fear of being laughed out of court. We have so many manuscripts of the New Testament, written so near the events themselves, that we can be sure of having the correct text somewhere in the manuscript tradition - and the differences are not more than minor ones. No single doctrine hangs on a disputed reading. Indeed, there is no ancient book where the manuscript tradition is so early and so widespread as is the case with the New Testament.

As the celebrated biblical archaeologist Kathleen Kenyon wrote, 'The interval between the date of the original composition and the earliest extent evidence becomes so small as to be negligible, and the last foundation for any doubt that the Scriptures have come down to us substantially as they were written has now been removed.'

• Can we trust what the Gospels contain? It is one thing to have reliable manuscripts. It is quite another to have reliable material about Jesus.

Here again we can be very confident. The Gospels are not primarily history or biography or teaching:

Many have put the Bible to the test of a lifetime's experience, and have found it a reliable guide.

they represent a new literary form, 'good news about Jesus'. That good news was preached all over the Empire in the thirty years before Mark, the earliest Gospel, was written. Does that interval not give opportunity for corruption and invention to creep in? No. Professor C.H. Dodd, in one of the most influential books on the New Testament this century, *The Apostolic Preaching and its Development*, has shown that much the same pattern of preaching about Jesus can be found in all the independent strands that go to make up the New Testament witness to Jesus.

Some of the events written in the Gospels are open to external verification: in each case they come through with flying colours. But there are two tests which are particularly helpful to modern scholars. One is the test of Aramaic. When something in the Gospels can easily be translated from its Greek dress back into the underlying Aramaic which Jesus and his disciples used, it proves very reliable. And yet these passages turn out to be all of a piece with the material which cannot so easily be translated back. Eastern people had long and accurate memories, and they tended to get it right. The second criterion is multiple attestation. If some event or saying is attested by several strands in the Gospels there is a high presumption of accuracy. And that applies to central reports like the main teaching of Jesus, the miracle of the feeding of the five thousand, Jesus' death and resurrection.

Although the subject of Gospel criticism is complex, it is true to say that no books in the world have been so minutely examined as the

Gospels over two-and-a-half centuries of scholarly criticism, and yet their credit stands today as high as ever.

• But what it really comes down to is this: can we trust the person on whom the Bible concentrates, Jesus Christ? Does the account of his life and teaching, his death and resurrection, his love and challenge ring true? Is he someone whom we not only admire but desperately need?

Many who declare the Bible to be unreliable are very ignorant of its teaching. But they are very sure that they do not want to take the costly step of giving in to Jesus Christ of whom that Bible speaks. It is not what they can't believe in the Bible which is the trouble, as Huck Finn once said, it is what they can believe! That is quite enough to face us with a massive moral hurdle. If the Bible is true, are we going to receive its truth?

MYTH 8

THERE IS NO EVIDENCE THAT JESUS CHRIST ROSE FROM THE DEAD

There is actually a great deal of evidence on this matter. There needs to be. Such an amazing claim ought not to be believed unless the evidence is overwhelming.

It is overwhelming! One erudite historian called the resurrection 'The best attested fact in ancient history.' Lord Chief Justice of England declared, 'The evidence for the resurrection of Jesus Christ from the dead is so strong that no intelligent jury in the world would fail to bring in a verdict that the resurrection story is true.'

Yet many close their minds to its possibility, let alone its truth. Some say, 'Resurrections don't happen. They are against nature.' But if there is a God who made everything and who is in control of this whole world, would i. really be beyond him to raise someone from the dead? Of course resurrections don't happen to every Tom, Dick and Harry. Indeed, the Bible claims that the resurrection of Jesus is totally unique. Nothing like it has ever happened before or since. He embodied the loving life of God in human flesh, and death,

Belief that Jesus rose from death brings with it certainty about life beyond the grave.

which is the last enemy for the rest of us, met its master in him.

There is a tremendous sense of triumph in the New Testament accounts of Jesus' resurrection. 'You crucified this Jesus,' said the apostle Peter in the very first Christian sermon, 'and killed him by the hands of lawless men. But God raised him up, having loosed the pangs of death because it was not possible for him to be held by it' (Acts 2.23f).

So what the Bible claims about Jesus is not some resuscitation, like the kiss of life after drowning; not some temporary extra span of life which would end in death anyhow. But rather that in Jesus of Nazareth, and in him alone, God's purpose for human life has been fully realized. After death he has been raised to a new quality, a new dimension of life. He is the first instalment of what is intended for us all. He is the pledge of human destiny for all who trust in him.

If it is true, this is the most amazing news the world has ever heard. It must mean that there is a God after all. It means that Jesus Christ really is his Son. It means that his death on the cross did not finish him. On the contrary, he is alive, and it is possible to meet him and be touched by his life and influence. If it is true, it means that we are not destined to go out like a light when we die, but that we are designed to know God and enjoy him for ever. It means that it is very important that we get to know him now, while we can. It means that we need not fear death in the way we once did. The act of dying may be unpleasant, but it will be marvellous to be dead, for that is 'to depart and to be with Christ which is far better'. So wrote Paul the apostle from prison as he himself faced the prospect of imminent death.

So the question of evidence is a very important one. A famous philosopher, Professor C.E.M. Joad, was once asked whom in past history he would most like to have met, and what he would most like to have asked him. His reply: 'I would most have liked to meet Jesus Christ, and I would have asked him, "Did you or did you not rise from the dead?".' Well, did he? Five vital points indicate that he did:

• Jesus really was dead. He was publicly executed before large crowds. He was certified as dead by both the centurion in charge of the execution and by the governor, Pilate, who sent to have the matter checked. Moreover, he has a spear pushed through his side just to make sure, and out came dark clot and pale serum, looking to the unsophisticated witness who records it like blood and water (John 19:34). There is no more certain legal-medical proof of death than that. Yes, Jesus was very dead that first Good Friday. The point would not be worth stressing were it not for the fact that some people, trying to evade the evidence for the resurrection, claim that Jesus was not really dead and revived in the cool of the tomb.

• The tomb was found empty. Jesus was buried in a new tomb, never before used, and therefore in mint condition and easily recognized (John 19.41). But when his friends went to tend his body after the intervening sabbath day, his body had gone; all

the accounts agree on this. This was utterly astonishing. His enemies had been working for years to
get him dead and buried. So they made very sure
of it and set a guard on the tomb and sealed an
enormous boulder over it (Matthew 27.62-66). It
made no difference. On Easter morning the tomb
was empty. (It is worth reading the accounts, in
Matthew 27.1-10; Mark 16.1-8; Luke 24.1-12;
John 20.1-18; 1 Corinthians 15.1-11).

That tomb was either emptied by men, or God
did in fact raise Jesus his Son from the grave.
But what men? You can discount his enemies.
They were only too glad he was out of the way.
Could his friends have removed the body? I think
not. They were very discouraged and expected no
such sequel to his death. And would they have
succeeded in turning the ancient world upside
down by proclaiming what they knew to be a lie,
a lie for which they were content to be torn apart
by lions in the arena? Read the story of the Acts
of the Apostles, and ask yourself if it rings false,
or whether these people were utterly convinced of
what they were saying.

• Jesus appeared after his death to many witnesses.
The New Testament never places undue stress on
the empty tomb. They were much more interested
in the living Jesus who overcame their very legiti-
mate doubts by appearing to them time and again
- in a garden, on a walk, in an upstairs room, by a
lake side. Each of the Gospels tells us about such
appearances (which lasted only forty days and then
ended as abruptly as they had begun). It is totally
implausible to consider them hallucinations: they

happened to hard-headed fishermen such as Peter as well as emotional women like Mary Magdalene, and civil servants such as Matthew. The resurrection appearances have never been satisfactorily explained away. They happened. And they demonstrate that Jesus is alive.

• The Christian Church owes its origin to the resurrection. Indeed, belief in the risen Christ was the first thing that distinguished the Christians from the other Jews. That belief brought the church into being and swept through the Roman Empire. That belief lights up the hearts of approximately a third of the human race twenty centuries after the events in question. It simply will not go away. It grows and spreads into every nation under the sun. Why? If it is not true it should have faded by now, instead of expanding all over the world.

• Many, many people have encountered the living Jesus, and been changed by him. It is not a matter of accepting one doctrine among many and defending it. It is a questions of personal experience. All down the ages from the first century to this there have been literally millions of people, like Saul of Tarsus, who turned right round from being totally opposed or totally indifferent to Christianity to being utterly convinced it is true. What changed them? They met with Jesus, alive, inviting them to respond in faith and challenging them to live his way. He changes people today, just as he changed the first disciples.

I have come to this life-changing encounter with him. And it is open to anyone willing to look in the right place. Where is that? In the Gospels; examine the evidence there. Look into the Christian community at worship, and catch the flavour. Look into what you can take in of Jesus Christ and say, 'Lord, if you are really alive, please make me sure of it. And then I am prepared to follow you whole-heartedly.' Many a doubter has found that such a prayer is answered.

MYTH 9

ALL THE EVIL AND SUFFERING IN THE WORLD PROVES THERE IS NO GOD.

Many people think that the problem of evil, with the suffering it brings, is an insuperable barrier to belief in a good God. The argument can be deployed like this.

● A God who is good and loving would not want to allow evil and suffering in his world.

● A God who is all-powerful could remove evil and suffering if he so desired.

● Therefore, if God is both good and powerful, there should be no evil or suffering.

● But undeniably there is evil and there is pain. So God (at least a good and powerful God) does not exist.

This argument is superficially impressive. But do those who ask for evil to be eradicated really think what they are asking? Just suppose for a moment that God were immediately to wipe out all evil. Where would we stand? Would not humanity be destroyed? For which of us is free from evil? Far from remaining an abstract, intellectual problem, evil is a very pressing moral problem within each one of us. We ourselves are the problem of evil. And if simple eradication were the answer, we would have no hope.

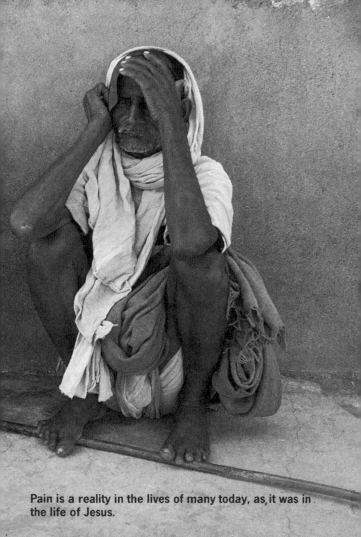

Pain is a reality in the lives of many today, as it was in the life of Jesus.

Or just suppose for a moment that the problem of pain and evil drives you to reject the existence of a loving God, and to imagine that some monster rules our destiny, or that the stars are in charge of our fortunes, how does that help? You may have got rid of one set of problems, but you have replaced them with a much bigger one. How do you explain kindness, goodness, love and humanity, unselfishness and gentleness in a world that is governed by a horrible monster or by the uncaring stars? Because life is not all evil. It is far more complex than that.

On any showing, evil and pain in the world constitute a massive problem both to belief and to behaviour. And Christianity offers no knock-down solution at a philosophical level. But the Bible does give us ground to stand on as we try to live in a world where suffering is real. Because it teaches us that God is no stranger to pain.

• The Bible teaches that God did not create evil and pain. The world he made was utterly good. But as early as that marvellous pictorial story of Adam and Eve we find humanity turning against God, using his gift of free will to rebel. And that brought the perfection of God's world tumbling down. Somehow there is a profound link between mankind and his environment. When humanity fell out of step with God and his purposes, and moral evil entered the world through that rebellion, suffering came in as well. The world is all of a piece: there cannot be evil without suffering. The Bible goes on to assert that behind human wickedness there lies a great outside influence, the devil, who hates God and everything to do with him. Jesus taught often about the reality of this evil force, who is out to spoil both mankind and his environment and do everything possible to attack God and his purposes of good. The Bible makes it plain that somehow this malign force is involved in the evil and suffering of this world. There is a war on between the forces of good and evil, and we are all caught up in that war every day. Such is the biblical teaching. Does it not ring true?

• Again, the Bible teaches that although God did not create evil and suffering, and although he does not will it, nevertheless he can and does use it. The presence of evil in the world has led many to strive for good. The presence of suffering in the world has produced qualities of character that would have been impossible without it - courage, endurance, self-sacrifice, compassion. . . God uses pain in a profound way to draw us to himself when normally we will not listen. In our pleasures he merely whispers. In our suffering he shouts.

• God did not leave us to stew in the mess we had made for ourselves. He became involved. He came to this world with all its sorrow and pain, its wickedness and entrenched evil. He came as a man among men. He lived in squalor and suffering. He knew thirst and hunger, flogging and heartbreak, fear and despair. He ended his life in one of the most excruciating of all deaths. So let nobody say that God does not care, and does not understand. He has personally gone through it all.

• God has dealt with the problem of evil and suffering at its root. Jesus not only shared our pain and agony on the cross. He took personal responsibility for the wickedness of every man or woman who has ever lived or ever will. He allowed that vast mountain of evil to crush him. And it cost him unspeakable suffering. It cost him hell. He cried out in anguish, 'My God, my God, why have you forsaken me?' By attacking the problem of evil which led to suffering, he was dealing with the problem of pain at its root. On the cross God willingly carried the evils of the whole world. We shall never understand it. We can only marvel at his fantastic self-sacrifice. God there experienced the problem of evil more intensely than any human being could possibly know. And he did it to free us from the cancer of evil which had invaded our deepest being.

• Lastly, God has overcome the problem of pain and evil. He has solved it, not as a mental problem but in its capacity to overwhelm us. The cross, and the resurrection which followed, are the standing evidence that evil and suffering do not have the last word in God's world. There is hope. For the cross was not the place of defeat, but of victory. On the first Good Friday Jesus died with a cry of triumph on his lips: triumph over pain and hatred, suffering and death, Satan and evil of every kind. And that first Easter Day he rose from the grip of death. Ever since then he has enjoyed the power of an endless life. Even death is a defeated foe.

And so the early Christians, and many of their successors ever since, have been able to see suffering not as an unmitigated evil, but as an opportunity to experience the victory of Jesus in their own lives.

And that victory shed a light on the dark recesses of evil and pain, even when they could not understand them. The victory of Jesus rising from the tomb was for them a pledge of their own destiny from evil and from pain. They could safely leave him to shed fuller light on it all in the life to come.

Christianity unashamedly looks beyond this life for the final solution of this mystery. But it does so confident that we have been given the key to the mystery in the cross and resurrection of Jesus Christ.

Christians believe in a suffering but overcoming God. And that belief prevents us from either becoming totally callous, or going out of our minds at all the suffering which afflicts our world.

MYTH 10

IT DOESN'T MATTER WHAT YOU BELIEVE. ALL RELIGIONS ARE BASICALLY THE SAME.

Of all the myths we have examined this seems the most charitable and sensible. It accords with the tolerance which is one of the virtues we cherish most. But on closer inspection it proves highly unsatisfactory.

In no other realm of life would we apply such an argument. What teacher would be satisfied with pupils who said, 'It does not matter what answer you give in algebra, Latin, history or geography. It all comes to the same thing in the end?' We may have multiple-choice questions today, but multiple answers? In religion as in everything else, we are called to judge which answers fit the facts.

Is it really likely that all religions lead to God, when they are so different, indeed so contradictory? In Hinduism the divine is plural and impersonal: the God of Islam is singular and personal; the God of Christianity is the Creator of the world; the divine of Buddhism is neither personal nor creative. You could scarcely have a greater contrast than that. Christianity teaches that God both forgives and assists us; in Buddhism there is no possibility of forgiveness and no hope of supernatural aid. The goal of all existence in Buddhism is *nirvana*, extinction, attained by the Buddha after no less than 547 births; the goal of all existence in Christianity is to know God and to enjoy him for ever. The use of images figures prominently in Hinduism; Judaism prohibits making any image of God. Islam allows a man four wives; Christianity one. Perhaps the greatest difference of all lies between the Bible which asserts that we can never save ourselves, try as we will; and all the other faiths which assert that a person will be saved, or reborn, or made whole, or achieve fulfilment by keeping teachings or living according to laws.

Nothing spells out this contrast more powerfully than comparing a Buddhist story with the very similar Parable of the Prodigal Son. In both, a boy comes home and is met by his father. But where the Prodigal Son is met with quite undeserved forgiveness and welcome, the Buddhist equivalent has to work off the penalty for his past misdeeds by years of servitude.

It does religion no service to pretend that all faiths are the same beneath some superficial clothing. They are not. They lead to radically different goals. Extinction or heaven; pardon, or paying it off; a personal God or an impersonal monad; salvation by grace or by works. The contrasts are irreconcilable.

Then why are so many people dedicated to such a shaky proposition?

• For several interesting reasons, the world has become a global village. Various faiths jostle one another just as various nationalities bump into one another in the streets. It is tacitly assumed that racial pluralism validates religious pluralism. But

71

it is a myth.

• Tolerance has reached such a stage that we assume God is a good, genial fellow. He will not blame us for our faults. Nobody could possibly be lost. But that too is a myth.

• Many act today as though faith in itself is what really matters. You have to believe in something, but it does not really matter what. That is another myth. Faith is like a rope. It matters enormously what you attach it to.

At Varanasi Hindus bathe in the holy river Ganges. The beliefs and practices of the major religions differ greatly. Each has its own integrity.

• And also, this approach means people can avoid decision. If all religions are the same, we don't have to choose. We'll be all right anyhow. But will we? What if that is another myth?

This easy assumption, that we are all looking for

God and will all find him in the end, is false both to what God is like and to human nature. If there is a God at all, then he is the source of ourselves and of our environment. He is Lord over all life. How can we puny human beings climb up to him? How can we comprehend him? Obviously, we can't. The only hope is that he may have somewhere shown us what he is like. The Bible, and only the Bible, claims that such a revelation has happened. Dimly at first, then with increasing light in the Old Testament, people began to see the truth of a God who loves us and speaks to us. And then the stage was set for God's final and decisive self-disclosure, in the coming of his Son. No longer is he the unknown God. 'No man has ever seen God, but the only begotten one, himself God, has made him known.' (John 1.18).

If the nature of God is one reason why the creature can never find his way to the Creator unaided, human nature is the other. The Bible tells us that we are essentially selfish, that we do not follow every gleam of light when we get it, but on the contrary we frequently turn our backs on the light and try to extinguish it. It tells us that there is a basic twist in human nature that makes us go wrong without our really trying.

If this is so, then we have no prospect of reaching God, and no religion can span the gulf between a holy God and us in our sinfulness. If there is to be any hope for us, there must be a divine rescue. Not only must God show us what he is like, but he must also find a way to have rebels back into his family, to reconcile enemies who want only to go their own way. The Bible, and the Bible alone, tells us that there is such a God and that he as found a way. The cross is the way by which God can justly forgive our sins and frailties: he has himself paid the penalty.

So you see Christianity is not really a religion at all, if by 'religion' you mean a way of trying to find God. It is a revelation and a rescue.

• It is a revelation of what God is like; and it comes in a form we can really take in, the form of a human life. It is also a revelation of what we are like, for men and women could not bear the purity of that life of Jesus but hounded him to the cross.

• It is also a rescue. God came to find me. And he met me in the death of his Son and beside the empty tomb from which his Son rose victorious.

Most amazing of all, this God, who provides both a revelation and a rescue instead of a religion, wants to meet me. He wants to relate to me in a personal way which even death will not be able to sever. No faith in the world is remotely comparable to this. All religions are not basically the same. It does matter very much what you believe.

·Does this mean that all other religions are totally wrong? Of course not. All have some measure of truth in them; the highest ones such as Islam and Judaism have a great deal of truth in them. They are like varied candles and lights in the darkness of the world. But they all pale into insignificance at the dawn. And the dawn has come with Jesus Christ. He fulfils the hopes and aspirations, the virtues and insights of whatever is true and good in all faiths.

ABANDON THE MYTHS. . . GO FOR THE TRUTH

The myths we have looked at in this book (and there are many like them) blind us to the truth as it is in Jesus. Truth can be painful, but if it really is the truth, it can never harm us. Here are five areas of Christian truth which I would encourage you to go for.

● Go for the truth about God. There are many pointers from within our world to the truth about God. And they tie in precisely with the sort of God the Bible tells us about: the God who made us, loves us, and communicates with us both by the Book of Nature and by the Book of Scripture.

● Go for the truth about Jesus. Jesus once claimed 'I am the truth', and there is everything in his life, teaching, death and resurrection to validate that astounding claim. Take a good long look at Jesus. He will not disappoint you, because he is the Truth.

● Go for the truth about yourself. You are an enigma, aren't you, even to yourself at times? You are a walking Civil War! At times so kind and thoughtful, generous and unselfish. At other times

There are no real intellectual obstacles to belief in Jesus. The way is open for us to put our trust in him.

so self-centred and vindictive, lustful and treacherous. What a contradiction I am, behaving now like a king, now like a pig. With the Roman poet Ovid I have to confess 'I see the better way and I approve it - but I follow the worse'. Optimists see the good things in human nature, and dream of utopia. Pessimists see little but moral squalor, political chaos and cosmic destruction ahead. Christianity sees us as like semi-ruined temples, still bearing marks of their original splendour. These temples need repair by the Architect who designed them. Jesus Christ is God's Architect for our lives. You need him, and he needs you, to be a building restored to its original beauty.

● Go for the truth about change. It is obvious that change is needed. It is obvious where change can come from. Very well then. Turn your ruined temple of a life over to the one who can restore it. It is basically a matter of letting him take over. Why not pray a prayer such as this?

Lord, I acknowledge that my life is far from what it ought to be. I admit that I have used excuse after excuse to keep you at arm's length. I realize that I need you very much to effect in me the changes which I cannot achieve by myself.

Lord, there is so much I don't understand about you. But I begin to see that you died on that awesome cross in order to deal with the evil in my life and the evil in the whole world. I believe you are risen and alive, and I want to meet you. Please come into my life